WORDS ARE CLOTHING

Poems and Pictures

To Rick
with love
Gudrun

GUDRUN

Note for Librarians: A cataloguing record for this book is available from Library and Archives Canada at www.collectionscanada.ca/amicus/index-e.html
ISBN 1-4120-7153-4

Printed in Victoria, BC, Canada. Printed on paper with minimum 30% recycled fibre.
Trafford's print shop runs on "green energy" from solar, wind and other environmentally-friendly power sources.

PUBLISHING™
Offices in Canada, USA, Ireland and UK

Book sales for North America and international:
Trafford Publishing, 6E–2333 Government St.,
Victoria, BC V8T 4P4 CANADA
phone 250 383 6864 (toll-free 1 888 232 4444)
fax 250 383 6804; email to orders@trafford.com
Book sales in Europe:
Trafford Publishing (UK) Limited, 9 Park End Street, 2nd Floor
Oxford, UK OX1 1HH UNITED KINGDOM
phone 44 (0)1865 722 113 (local rate 0845 230 9601)
facsimile 44 (0)1865 722 868; info.uk@trafford.com
Order online at:
trafford.com/05-2048

10 9 8 7 6 5 4 3 2

for Robert

Notes From The Author

These poems are, intentionally, not in topical or chronological order. Rather, they are meant to reflect the many moods of life, ever-changing, sometimes dramatically, other times capriciously - always "One Day At A Time".

My fifth grade teacher, Miss Anna Arnova, was the first of many who taught me that poems are best appreciated when read aloud. I pass this tip along to you.

To my family - especially my children, to my friends - many of them "anonymous", and to The Bluebird, my thankful heart acknowledges your enormous contribution to my understanding of life. You have been, collectively and individually, a shining example. For this blessing and for your unconditional love, I offer my gratitude.

Special thanks to Vickie DeWitt for her technical assistance, constant support and encouragement.

There's a bluebird on my shoulder
And there's a bluebird in my heart
     He was there when I was born
     He'll be there when I depart
He sings to me in the morning
And he lulls me to sleep at night
     He's there when things go wrong
     He's there when all is right
There's a bluebird on my shoulder
And there's a bluebird in my heart

Words Are Clothing

I swear it's so
I didn't know
    that you were there
    someplace, somewhere
    that all the while
    I saved my smile
I swear it's so
I didn't know
    that you would come
    and make life fun
    that I could be
    filled with sweet glee
I swear it's so
I didn't know
    that I would dare
    that I would care
    but this is true
    really, I knew

Words Are Clothing

I dislike saying I'm sorry
Because I know it's just not true
Perhaps I'm shameless, amoral
But there it is: I do not rue

I accept the consequence
Of all I say and all I do
The critics will not sway me
I'm stuck with it: I do not rue

Sometimes I falter, even err
And find that I must start anew
Determined, I go from there
And still insist: I do not rue

I think it's a waste of my time
And a waste of my effort, too
I simply cannot feel regret
For it's a fact: I do not rue

Yes, my mother lives in Brooklyn
On Congress Street and that's a fact
And yes, she is pushing ninety
She's eighty-nine, to be exact
It's March and still cold and windy
And she says to me with a smile
"I'm suffr'ing from cabin fever
Let's go out and walk for a while"
We bundle up and off we go
Two of us and one shopping cart
It's a cold day but the sun shines
And warms the cockles of her heart
"I know where there's a daffodil,
One ready to burst into bloom"
And we're pulled in that direction
By the scent of Spring's sweet perfume

→

Words Are Clothing

"I know where there are some crocus
What a lovely purple they are"
Down one street and up another
She smiles and says it's not far
"I know where there are some snow drops
They always take my breath away"
And off we go in search of more
Of nature's generous array
"I know where there's Stellaria
That's chick weed, if you didn't know"
And so our walk continues on
And my mother is all aglow
An hour and a half later
We arrive back where we began
Dear Mother, you are amazing
No wonder I'm your biggest fan

Words Are Clothing

sitting in the sun
really is such fun

warming up my toes
burning up my nose

feeling mighty good
cause i know i should

and when i am done
i'll be on the run

so let me relax
before i make tracks

It's the place to be
come and be with me

She has your name
     She shares your bed
I have two roses
     that are red
You have a life
     that cannot include me
I have your red roses
     and I am free
We all must live
     with what God imposes
But, ah, I'm the one
     who has the roses

Words Are Clothing

You boggle my mind
You awe my senses
You can be unkind
You stun defenses
So, why do I love
Against odds so high
Hey, You-Up-Above
Could you tell me . . . WHY?

Celebrate the strange
Own the beast
Name the storm
Welcome the feast

Words Are Clothing

O, Angels darling, Angels dear
As Shakespeare said "Lend me your ear"
I need to hear blessed voices
I need to make proper choices
I vow to listen with my heart
So, Angels dear, please do your part

Truth stares at me
And I stare back
    My heart is cold
    My mood is black
I turn from Him
Deny Him room
    Then I give space
    To the dark gloom
How sad for me
For I do know
    That on this path
    There's no rainbow

Wake up! Wake up! my lover said
As we lay side by side in bed
And then, without another word
He turned me into a bluebird
It's true! It's true! I'm not lying
In an instant, I was flying !!

Words Are Clothing

Yo! are you a whiz?
If so, here's a quiz
First, tell me, my dove
Are you yet in love?
Do sweet dreams come true?
Is the sky still blue?
Hope? Is it alive?
When will peace arrive?
Have all tears been shed?
Are roses still red?
Does God provide all?
Will we hear His call?
Is there time to mend?
Or is this the end?

Why didn't I take one step at a time?
I did not act in a manner sublime
My reason collided with rationale
And the thing that suffered was my morale
I ran too fast, tripped and fell on my face
Disqualified myself from the Big Race
Bloody and breathless, I've laid a long time
And my life resembles a pantomime
I'm "missing in action", both night and day
Don't know what I do, don't hear what I say
I need to rise up from this pit of pain
To hear my heart beat, to wake up my brain
So let me speak up now and take a stand
And pray for a life more noble and grand

Words Are Clothing

There is a space
between

sanity and insanity

that
is room enough for me

God is Spirit, as am I
    was not born and cannot die
God is Soul. He gives the spark
    that leads the way out of dark
God is Wisdom and His might
    is my comfort and my light
God is Life, each breath I take
    God, my all, asleep, awake
God is Love, His gift divine
    Freely given, it is mine
God is Truth, eternally
    Where there is truth, God will be
God is Constant, evermore
    He is my strength and my core
God is All, my everything
    The Child, the Man and the King

Daisies are white
    and leaves are green
Pepper is hot
    and love is mean
Still, you are mine
    though you think not
And memories
    are all I've got
Life goes on and
    takes me along
And I must sing
    a sad love song

all
of
life
is
possible
with

========================

G O D ' S G R A C E

========================

and
with
faith
and
trust
this
truth
I
embrace

Here's the pen

    I have the yen

I have the time

    WHERE'S THE RHYME???

Be with me in every thought , word and deed
Be with me, dear God, in my time of need
Be with me in the decisions I make
Be with me, sweet Lord, with each step I take
Be with me and give me a clearer view
Be with me and let me represent you

O ! Joy, where have you gone
My sweet, why did you leave?
I've lost all touch with you
And all alone, I grieve

My whole world has turned gray
There is no black or white
My eyes are dimmed by tears
I cannot see the light

Come back to me, dear friend
And stay with me the while
And, please, I beg of you
Return at once my smile

Words Are Clothing

Words are clothing for the thoughts
    that run around naked in my mind
I dress them up and take them out
    so that they may become
better acquainted with me and my world

They say that thought is mother to the deed
I say cause is father to the outcome
And remember this when you plant the seed
It is hard to be greater than the sum

Hang on, Goody-Two-Shoes !

You're heading for a wall
You're heading for a fall
I think you're tempting fate
I think it's way too late

Words Are Clothing

I'm sitting here upon a rock
One of many that form a dock
Out of the corner of my eye
I see a yellow butterfly
Come rest a moment; be with me
And like the butterfly, be free

Words Are Clothing

Go away everyone
Leave me alone I pray
I've given all I've got
I wish you wouldn't stay
I gave it willingly
I did it in Love's name
I wish for you God's peace
I wish for me the same
For now, I need quiet
And time to heal and rest
To hear my God tell me
He knows I did my best

I left you
    I know not why

I left you
    I said goodbye

I left you
    All day I sigh

I left you
    All night I cry

I left you
    I know not why

A dentist's office
     is a weird place
With an air of ether
     and pain
How intriguing
     The people are calm
Waiting to be drilled
     does not seem sane

"Hey, how's it going ?" they all ask
"Oh, I'm O.K." is my reply
They can't see I'm wearing a mask
They don't know I'm telling a lie
Outer me seems to be in place
Inner me has been ripped apart
And there's a smile upon my face
That can't reflect what's in my heart
The hurt I feel is so intense
I pray for God to give me ease
I offer up my sad laments
Hoping He will honor my pleas

I stare at your picture
Remembering your smile
And it has the power
Still and yet to beguile
Fond mem'ries embrace me
And I return your smile
We gaze at each other
And love lingers the while

Words Are Clothing

How dreadful is that monster Doubt
Who creeps upon me unawares
I find his presence has the clout
To disturb my dreams and my prayers
His winds across my garden blow
Scattering his prolific seeds
Fed by mistrust, they start to grow
And Eden is choked by the weeds

Words Are Clothing

I'm tired and cold
    down to my marrow
I've strayed too far
    from the path so narrow
My brain is wired
    and my nerves are frayed
I'm right in the midst
    of the mess I've made
I'm weary and pooped
    beyond all reason
I don't know and don't care
    what the season

→

I'm tired pf playing
the game to win
Tired of not knowing
what state I'm in
Tired of travel
to distant places
Tired of new towns
and stranger's faces
And I'm tired of
being sad and blue
But, O! my love
I'm not tired of you

When I am blind and cannot see

the truth right there in front of me

I need to turn to God with plea

for only He can set me free

Let your eyes
    search me
        with question
Daring answer
    to yield
        and bend
And the future
    calls
        to mention
The hope that
    the heavens
        do send

Words Are Clothing

Peace, be my constant companion
My Friend, my Savior and my Lord
Give me new and deeper meaning
Into the truth that is Your word
My soul yearns for serenity
For calm to hold fast in my life
And I need a faith to cling to
When days are filled with stress and strife
My God is called the Prince of Peace
Yet it matters not what His name
Only that I know in my heart
Peace and God are one and the same

Words Are Clothing

Roses are red
Violets are blue
Moustaches are
Tasty to chew

Cold hands
Warm heart
Cold feet
Warm fart

How frivolous you are !

What a wonderful word is frivolous
It rhymes so very well with syllabus
It's a word with onomatopoeia
And that rhymes nicely with diarrhea

I press my nose to the window

I see only darkness

Yet, all is not lost

It cools my nose

NOSE, NOSE, ANYTHING GOES !

Words Are Clothing

What do I do
    with the leftover love

And all the sweet dreams
    I must get rid of

Should I give them to God
    with hope that He

Will recycle and
    refund them to me

Running and restless and hiding
Not from you, rather from myself
Matters of the heart are biding
Indeed, my life is on the shelf
I cannot run any longer
I've gone as far as I can go
I'm weak and yearn to be stronger
I'm weary of the sound of NO
I want some moments of quiet
When war wages not in my soul
I long for a golden sunset
I ache to understand my role

MY FATHER CAME TO ME
　　in a moment sweet
　　on memory's feet
and his loving smile
said "I'll stay a while"

MY FATHER CAME TO ME
　　and his voice so calm
　　was a loving balm
and my grateful heart
knows we're not apart

My back is to the wall
It makes it hard to fall
I must be very still
I can I should I will
A voice within me cries
"Don't even blink your eyes.
Turn off all of your brain.
Deny all of your pain."
God whispers in my ear
"Don't panic. Have no fear.
I'll do what you can't do
And all is right and true."

The anger is gone
    and replaced by tears
My soul is wounded
    and filled with fears
The anger is gone
    it fled in the night
Confused and perplexed
    I don't know what's right
There is no firm ground
    here under my feet
The pain in my heart
    makes sorrow complete

→

I long to be back
    in His loving arms
I want to deserve
    the warmth of His charms
But I am impaled
    by guilt and remorse
I've strayed from the path
    of God's righteous course
Get down on your knees
    O, child of regret
For He forgives all
    or did you forget?

O, Sun, why did you flee
Behind that mountain cloud
Come out and shine on me
I'll sing your praises loud

Ah, now the clouds depart
Here comes the sun anew
He wraps me in his arms
And smiles upon me, too

Thank you for your blessing
You do it with such ease
O, Mighty Golden Sun
Keep shining on me, please

Words Are Clothing

It is spring in my heart
    and through the snow
Left by the winter
    of my discontent
Come the slender leaves
    and fragile blossoms
Of the sprightliest of blooms:
    the crocus
And as I smile
    at their audacity
I am awed
    that I was wise enough
to plant the bulbs in my garden
    last autumn

O, little girl, calm down
Doomsday is not yet here
In point of fact, dear one
It isn't even near
Comfort and help are yours
The good news is...He's here...
He fills you with His hope
He whispers "Do not fear"
Give a sigh of relief
And smile...He wants you to...
Come and sit on my lap
O, yes, I do mean YOU !

It's time to remember again
That, indeed, God does have a plan
And it's been in operation
Since before man and time began
The Lord's plan works to perfection
The only thing it needs from me:
An attitude of gratitude
And faith to an endless degree

Ev'ry time I dare to think
    that I am over you
I stumble upon feelings
    that were hidden from view
Perhaps I am mistaken
    to think that love can die
Perhaps love is like the clouds
    that gather in the sky
Clouds have their destiny
    Even as love has its fate
And it is the soothing rain
    that washes clean the slate
Then thru the grace of God's plan
    the love and clouds reshape
It is an endless cycle
    from which there's no escape

But, really, what was I to do?
I had no idea what bugged you
When did the good feelings depart?
Why did you tramp upon my heart?
Why do you say the things you say?
Could it have played another way?
What was all that darkness about?
Why did you behave like a lout?
Where, O! where did all the love go?
These are the things I'd like to know
Questions are many...answers few
This I know...I give up on you!

Words Are Clothing

How lovely to be quiet
    and wait upon your smile
How lovely to be quiet
    and think of you the while
And in that silence
    I hear more
Than I have ever heard
    before
Your smile gives wings
    to words not said
And with sweet joy
    two hearts are wed

Words Are Clothing

My winter of discontent
                is ending
And my broken heart, at last
                is mending
For the memory of your warm
                brown eyes
Eases my pain and erases
                your lies

Integrity lives within
    Where else could it start?
It is the living proof
    of the beating of my heart

Words Are Clothing

I've heard it said
　　that love is blind
They speak of trust
　　in the same kind
How odd it is
　　I cannot see
What shapes my live
　　and destiny

Words Are Clothing

O, why have I let go of Love
And traveled to the Land of Fear
How foolish of me not to see
That all of my Angels are near
Take with you all doubt, gloom and pain
And go away, O! Monster Black
And let me make this very clear
Don't dare bother to come back!

Words Are Clothing

Search under rocks

Look to the stars

Scan the heavens

Set sail for Mars

the noisy me
    must first be soothed
before serenity
    is mine
and i've begun to know
    that peace
is sweeter
    than the finest wine

Words Are Clothing

I wish that trees could talk to me
And tell me what they feel and see
Weeping willows could share their pain
Standing in beauty in the rain
Ginkgoes could speak with pride of roots
For theirs are the oldest of shoots
Crab apples could talk in a snit
They'd be sullen and have a fit
Spruces bragging of being neat
And they should be proud of that feat
Pine trees could groan and they could moan
So sad because they are alone

→

Wild cherries could tell of their sprees
Be the envy of other trees
Aspens don't stutter but they quake
And I could ask them if they ache
Saguaros could act snippety
Because they are very prickly
Yes, I'd listen to the dogwood
The maple, the oak, the redwood
The elm, the cypress and the beech
The chestnut, the apple and peach
I'd listen to them all with glee
It's so easy to love a tree

Words Are Clothing

Hope and hurt have collided
head on
and left me numb and senseless
Tears are trapped in the
receptacle
that is my heart
My soul and spirit are racked
with pain
And yet, I swear, somewhere,
beyond this,
I hear laughter and I feel
a smile

Fly away, wasp
I'm not a rose

Get off my pen !
Get off my nose !

Let me sit and
enjoy the rays

It's one of nature's
perfect days

If only doing the right thing
Was always easy and felt good
Yes, if only it was easy
Then I know I could when I should
But there are times when it's so hard
To walk the straight and narrow road
There are those days when honesty
Feels like a heavy, awesome load

Words Are Clothing

God, tell me what to do
I need to hear from you
What to think? What to feel?
Should I pray? Should I kneel?
What to do? What to say?
I need orders...today!!
From your mouth to my ear
Talk to me. Make it clear
Count on me to obey
To live my life Your way

Quickly flows the river of life
Filled to the brim with joy and strife
It does not stop; it does not rest
Running endlessly in its quest
And futile it is to ask why
For whether we laugh or we cry
The river glides along its way
Mile unto mile and day by day
It is wise to go with the flow
Let it take us where it will go
Yes, float on it and hope and dream
And learn a lesson from the stream

I'm so weary of feeling down
AND I'M SO TIRED OF THIS FROWN

I want a smile upon my face
I WANT A DOSE OF MY GOD'S GRACE

O! Blessed, dear Divinity
LIFT ME OUT OF MY MISERY

I want to rise up and be tall
HEY, LET'S GO SHOPPING AT THE MALL !

A SURVIVAL PLAN

inch by inch

mile . . . . by . . . . mile

pinch by pinch

smile . . . . by . . . . smile

Words Are Clothing

up above

They say that Heaven is

and Hell is somewhere
down below

Is Earth, then, the place in-between

the height of joy

and

the depth of woe?

I don't believe that dreams can die
Whoever said that told a lie
It's just not true that they can end
For they can change and they can bend
They can take on new shape and form
And they can weather any storm
For their beauty lies in their strength
And they will go to any length
They will rise above pain and grief
They'll endure scorn and disbelief
They'll go underground if need be
The one thing they won't do is flee
Thunder, lightning, sleet, rain or hail
It doesn't matter...they'll prevail
I don't believe that dreams can die
Whoever said that told a lie

I never sought fortune
  yet it has sought me out
I never wanted fame
  of that I have no doubt
Neither wealth nor good looks
  could ever be my aim
Nor do I seek to be
  the keeper of the flame
All I ever wanted
  was peace within my heart
For God to rule supreme
  for me to do my part

Words Are Clothing

It really would be such a crime

If I sat here and took the time

To dedicate to you a rhyme

It seems your tastes are more sublime

Say, would you like some pantomime?

Words Are Clothing

Don't be a chump

Make the big jump

Over the hump

Then play your trump

Be quiet Be still
I can and I will
Be brave and be true
What else can I do?
Believe without end
Be my own best friend
Be happy and smile
And after a while
Though it may feel odd
Let go and let God

Our paths parted abruptly and sadly
    with a finality quite clear
Honestly, I loved you madly
    and I have shed many a tear
But, really, my nature insists
    that I bid you a fond farewell
For I have been sad long enough
    and it's time to heal and be well
I'd say it was loads of fun
    but you and I know that's not true
So "Goodbye.God bless you.Please.Move.
    There's someone in back of you!"

I cannot force rhyme or reason
I cannot rush time or season
I cannot change what God has planned
I cannot change a grain of sand

God, come into my heart
and thaw it, please
God, take over my mind
and give it ease
God, live within my soul
and make me whole

your brown eyes
smile
on
me
and I feel the warmth
of the sun petals
that
surround
you

Come yield to me
    though it be an excess
And allow my love
    your fears to undress
Let our passion be
    the burning incense
That blinds us
    to every consequence
I long to take you
    to my wilderness
I ache to know
    your touch of tenderness
I pray that my heart's
    gentle eloquence
Overcomes, at last,
    your ev'ry defense

Do you find my poems amusing?

Are they witty? Are they bright?

Do you find that you recall them

In the middle of the night?

Words Are Clothing

Go away ! Go away !
  man in my brain
You take up too much space
  You give me pain
Do you have a name?
  Do you have a face?
Leave ! Do your tap dancing
  some other place
You disturb my sanity
  and my wits
Leave me alone, sir
  I don't need these fits

Chaos has its own beauty
    No snowflake is like another
Each leaf has its own pattern
    Every star is a planet

I recognize the uniqueness
    of all of God's universe
And one cell, one cause unites me
    with all that it is

Words Are Clothing

My lover's touch
can do so much
　　It fans the fire
　　of my desire

My lover's eyes
are warm and wise
　　They see the me
　　I long to be

My lover's arms
convey his charms
　　Enfolding me
　　in ecstasy

Words Are Clothing

Clearly, I see
    I've been set free
By God's decree
    He heard my plea
And granted me sobriety
    To keep this gift
These things I do
    Adore my God
Give praises, too
    Look for God's will
Let go of mine
    Believe there is
A plan divine
    Forgive myself
When I forget
    Avoid the trap
Of sad regret
    Remember that
God has a plan
    To make all right
I can't. He can.

The day was sweet, the sky was blue
And God was clearly in my view
When suddenly it all turned black
And with a roar, I went off track
Anger became my only thought
In a flash I was distraught
I was seduced by all of it
I was outraged. I had a fit
Forgetting to love or to pray
My serenity flew away

→

But, in time, I stopped and stood still
And my arms reached up to the sky
"O, God, help me to know your will"
And from my soul, came a deep sigh
First, God took away the hatred
And then God took away the fear
And when those two monsters had fled
Then did the anger disappear
My attitude began it's change
And soon surrender was in sight
Thanks be to the grace of my God
Who comforts me with Faith and Light

Words Are Clothing

Come warm my toes

And feed my soul

Build stairs to go

From my black hole

Words Are Clothing

Believe me when I tell you I'm
Mature enough to handle "NO"
And the point of this little rhyme
Is to convince you that it's so
For openers, I will confess
I much prefer to hear a "YES"
For positive replies are great
And negatives I really hate
Like everyone I get my share
Some Yesses here and some Noes there
When things go my way I can smile
And feel uplifted for a while
But when ev'ry door is shut tight
And nothing but nothing goes right
When I am face to face with "NO"
And start to feel unhappy woe
That's when I say to me "Dear one
Life isn't just all games and fun
And if you're never, ever sad
How will you know when you are glad?"

Words Are Clothing

as a rule
i'm no fool

    but i slip
    and i trip

and i get
dripping wet

    dry me, sun
    i'm gudrun

as a rule
i'm no fool

Words Are Clothing

Balderdash, rot and fooey, rats and blats
I'm weary of wearing so many hats
I'm sick of understanding, being good
Tired of doing what I know I should
I don't want the hurt...I don't want the pain
I'm bored with the sun...I'm bored with the rain
Turn off the music and make time stand still
I've lost my energy...I've lost my will
Don't know what happens next or when or where
And here's the bottom line...I just don't care

O, paradise is not a place
that I shall ever find
For it is not geography
it is a state of mind

Life is a ball

So stand up tall

And have the gall

To want it all

Should I believe in my feelings?

Should I move over and make room?

And, Is this really happening?

Do I know or do I presume?

Compared to the woe of heartache
    physical pain's a piece of cake
My back's a mess and hurts like hell
    but other than that, all is well

Brief Ode To Time

Sometimes I deny you
Sometimes you assault me
At times, you are my friend
    but often (too often)
    you are the enemy
I curse you when you hang heavy
    and
I curse you when you fly by
    without me
Time eternal...
    ....you fill me with awe and fear
Your limitations, which exist
    only in my mind,
astound my need to be free
Time, I salute you
    On occasion, you have
    vanquished me
In rare moments, I find myself
    at peace with you

Words Are Clothing

I disliked saying I'm sorry
And now I see that it was true
I was shameless and amoral
And here it is: I do, too, rue

I did not accept the results
Of all I did and all I said
I behaved outrageously
I'm stuck with it: my face is red

Yes, I still falter, even err
And find that I must start anew
And I can grow in love if I
Forgive myself and others, too

The years have aged and mellowed me
And how changed is my testament
When I am wrong, it is wiser
To acknowledge it and repent.

First she stops, then stands still
Soon comes a slow, sweet smile
For there he is again
To be with her a while
He pops into her mind
In the blink of an eye
He lights and then he flits
Just like the butterfly
Those moments are delight
That fill her heart and soul
And joy and peace are hers
And perfect love her goal

Words Are Clothing

come with me and fly
    to the mountain high
we shall dwell above
    the demands of love
and we'll soar like birds
    where we need no words
you can be just you
    and do what you do
and I can be me
    we can both be free
you can fly away
    I can choose to stay
no promise...no vow
    we live in the now

When I'm not filled with love so dear
Then I am filled with awesome fear
The choice is always mine to make
It's me who picks the path I take
I can resist these simple facts
Live in denial and be lax
Or I can choose to change my ways
And live in peace...Oh, happy days

A little while ago
Your presence came to me
A miracle occurred
And it set our love free
Not a word was spoken
There wasn't any sound
Even so I heard you
The silence was profound
Your eyes searched and found me
Our hearts were opened wide
The truth was there to see
It had no place to hide
Love has worked its magic
God has invoked His will
And we shall meet again
When both our hearts are still

HOW TO

<u>P</u>ray and give thanks for my sobriety

<u>R</u>ejoice in my daily reprieve from alcoholism

<u>O</u>ffer the love and grace I receive to others

<u>C</u>are about myself and care about others

<u>E</u>agerly believe in the Promises of AA

<u>E</u>arnestly work the Twelve Steps

<u>D</u>are to be (reasonably) happy

Hey ! I don't have the "blues"
I'm pleased as I can be
And if you should find them
Don't send them back to me
I feel like a bluebird
Such freedom ! Such sweet bliss !
I'm certain that I can fly
I could get used to this

INDEX

I don't believe that dreams can die - 85
I left you - 35
I never sought fortune - 86
I press my nose - 49
I stare at your picture - 38
I swear it's so - 4
I wish that trees could talk to me - 72, 73
If only doing the right thing - 79
I'm sitting here upon a rock - 33
I'm so weary of feeling down - 82
I'm tired and cold - 40, 41
Integrity lives within - 67
It's time to remember again - 62
It is spring in my heart - 57
It really would be such a crime - 87
I've heard it said - 68
Let your eyes search me - 43
Life is a ball - 113
My back is to the wall - 53
My father came to me - 52
My lover's touch - 101